FREYA STARK IN THE LEVANT

Freya Stark at her home in Asolo

MALISE RUTHVEN

FREYA STARK
IN THE LEVANT

GARNET PUBLISHING

Text copyright ©1994 Malise Ruthven
Photographs copyright © 1994 St Antony's College Middle East Centre
Design copyright © Garnet Publishing Ltd

First Edition

ISBN: 1 85964 003 6

British Library Cataloguing-in-Publication Data.
A catalogue record for this book is available from the British Library.

The photographs of Freya Stark on pages 2, 10, 11 and 14 are
reproduced courtesy of John Murray (Publishers) Ltd, with grateful
thanks.

Design by Elizabeth van Amerongen.
Cover design by Arthur op den Brouw.
House editor Anne Watson.
Typeset by Columns Ltd, Reading.
Reproduction by Creative Color Typographical Solutions Ltd, London
Printed in the Lebanon.

Published by Garnet Publishing Ltd,
8 Southern Court, South Street,
Reading RG1 4QS, UK.

CONTENTS

N.B. Pre-1946 Borders

INTRODUCTION

From her earliest childhood Freya Stark was destined to become a traveller. Born in Paris in 1893 to parents both of whom were artists, she was brought up between Devon, London and northern Italy. Having a German grandmother, she was already speaking four languages by the age of seven. An accident just before her thirteenth birthday tore away half her scalp and mutilated one of her ears spoiling, in her own words, "such looks as I might have had". She received no formal education until she entered Bedford College (now part of London University) at the age of eighteen. Up till then her knowledge of European literature had been acquired haphazardly from family and friends. Before she could take her degree the First World War had broken out. Determined to get as near as possible to the action, she volunteered as a nurse on the Italian-Austrian front. She assisted at amputations and witnessed the famous Italian retreat from Caporetto in 1917. She was a keen mountaineer, and after the war climbed both the Matterhorn and Monte Rosa. The experience of dangling at the end of a rope thousands of feet above a valley in the Dolomites gave her the sense, which she never lost, of triumphing over danger. "The clutch of fear left as if it were a knot being untied."

Freedom from fear – not just of physical danger, but of social embarrassment – was one of the keys to her success as a traveller. Part of it was due to her unusual cosmopolitan upbringing. Although her parents were both English (in fact, they were first cousins) her mother had been brought up in Italy. Freya and her sister always spent part of the year there, at their grandmother's house in Genoa or at the home of their father's friend, Herbert Young, in the beautiful renaissance town of Asolo near Venice. As comfortably off bohemians – in today's terms, "well-heeled hippies" – Freya's parents were liberal in outlook, sophisticated in manners and free from the social constraints that bedevilled most English people in matters of class and gender. Long treks on Dartmoor or in the Dolomites prepared her not only for the physical rigours of travelling in rough places, but for encounters with country people. Italy at the turn of the century was "undeveloped" in much the same way as the eastern Mediterranean would be in the 1920s and 1930s. Writing from the Lebanon in 1928 she noted the similarities: "It is all very like Italy in some ways. The Mediterranean is one family." At a time when most English people tended to be shy or mistrustful of "natives", more concerned with maintaining their dignity as members of a ruling caste than meeting people on common ground, she approached people from all backgrounds directly and without self-importance. Her very distinctive brand of imperialism was free from feelings of racial superiority; rather it was based on the platonic ideal of government by a class of disinterested administrators. The vision may have been naïve, but she fought for it consistently, often incurring suspicion or downright hostility for "going native" from the British circles she tended to idealize. If she sometimes romanticized the people she encountered, she did so from proximity. Her travel books – especially the earlier ones – are as much about people as places. She had an artist's eye for details of manners and dress, a novelist's talent for re-inventing dialogue. She experienced the real life of the people – the

Flora Stark painted
by her husband

poverty, disease, the chronic insecurity of feuding clans – in a way that few male travellers, obsessed with achieving their goals, were able to do. She exploited her relative poverty and vulnerability, knowing that in the Islamic world where she mostly travelled, the pilgrim or supplicant brought out the best in people, and that this was the surest guarantee of protection. It was a role most Europeans, and especially the British, would find difficult, if not impossible, since social prestige and honour depended on being seen to "pay one's way". She believed that the worst thing a traveller could do was to scatter money about. "We insult and corrupt people by treating their goodness as if it could be paid for . . . Nothing is more subtly insulting than to refuse to be under an obligation."

The qualities that made Freya Stark such an impressive travel writer also made her a good photographer. She was not, it has to be said, among the great photographers: she had neither the patience, nor the technical proficiency to record images that would consistently match the descriptive power of her writing. But she possessed two talents that made it possible for her to produce interesting, sometimes exceptional, pictures. One was the ability to talk people into letting her photograph them. The Islamic world has a long iconophobic tradition whose roots lie in a religious hostility to the sin of "idolatry". Until recent times this was thought to include any representation of human or animal forms. Photography was by no means as generally accepted as it is today, when most of the countries of the Middle East have been exposed to various forms of mass tourism, not to mention the domestic varieties of photography practised by local people or returning emigrés. Skill and charm of a high order were needed to obtain even passable images, especially of people. A photographer will always attract attention, inviting hostility or suspicion. Many of her best pictures were obtained using a form of subterfuge employed by many photographers in the region. She would line up a shot of an innocent arch or old building just like any tourist, and wait for an unsuspecting subject to walk into the picture. Her other gift was an excellent eye for composition, doubtless inherited from her artist parents. From her upbringing in Italy, she knew and understood the grammar of painting. Her pictures are sometimes less than sharp. They are nearly always well-balanced, whether of people or landscape. They record a world that, through war, modernization and development, has largely disappeared. Where buildings remain as they were in her pictures – as in the souks of Aleppo, or the wonderful "desert

Freya Stark aged 10 months with her father

Manhattans" of the Wadi Hadhramaut – people no longer dress as they did. Camel transport has all but gone, even in the Arabian heartlands; great cities like Hama and Beirut have changed beyond recognition as a result of rebellion and civil war. Ancient sites – like the Greek cities of Anatolia or Petra in Jordan – have succumbed to mass tourism, losing those poignant, evanescent qualities that Freya liked to dwell upon when she contrasted past glories with present squalor and meditated on the transitoriness of civilization. In photography as in travel, her sex was often a positive advantage. While men often enjoyed being photographed, they were inclined to resist the idea of images of their womenfolk being "taken away", especially by a stranger. The veil worn in public renders women symbolically invisible: and though complete veiling is not formally enjoined by the Qur'an, the idea of female invisibility is deeply bound up with notions of the sacred. The word *harām*, meaning taboo or forbidden, has the same Arab root as *harīm*, the portion of the traditional Muslim household reserved for women and *haram*, a sacred precinct, as in al-Haram al-Sharif, the "Noble Sanctuary" in Jerusalem. When she was by herself, Freya had little difficulty in persuading women to allow her to photograph them. When men were present, it was an entirely different matter: "We wanted to take photos of Druse women," she recounts in one of her *Letters from Syria*, "but of course when they saw us not only

Freya Stark in her forties

with men but with policemen, they fled even before we got near to them."

From her first expedition to the Levant until her trips to Yemen and the Himalayas in the 1970s Freya was never without her camera. She estimated that she spent up to a quarter of her travelling time on photography. In order to preserve her films from the heat, she would rise before dawn to process them, feeding the rolls by feel into a bakelite tank inside a black developing bag. She had the printing done by a commercial photographer in Treviso on her return to Italy. Many of the pictures were used to illustrate her books. During the 1970s she made a new selection of prints. She had them bound into eighty-odd volumes and captioned them herself. Memory was already beginning to fade, and not all her captions are consistent with the accounts of her movements contained in her published writings. Where discrepancies exist, I have corrected them, relying on her correspondence to determine where she happened to be at any given time.

The collection she bequeathed to St Antony's College contains some 5,000 mounted prints and about ten times that number of negatives. The earliest negatives, about 100 of them dating from 1927–8, are on conventional 120 roll film; but the vast majority are on 35mm and were taken with the Leica III camera she bought in Berlin in 1933 and used for the rest of her career. The camera, a favourite with travellers between the wars, was small and robust, with a variety of interchangeable lenses. Freya Stark preferred to use a 35mm/f3.5 wide angle lens to the standard 50mm Elmar lens supplied with the camera. As well as providing a wider angle, this lens has excellent depth of field, permitting foreground and background to remain in focus. She used a yellow/green type "G" screw-in filter permanently with this lens, whatever the light conditions. For portraits and other close-ups she used a 90mm/f4 Elmar lens. Apart from the lenses the only other accessory she carried was a torpedo-shaped multi-frame "Vidom" viewfinder. She carried this in her handbag and would often compose her pictures with it before bringing out the camera.

The oldest pictures in this volume date from the winter of 1927-8, when Freya Stark stayed for three months with the Quaker Mission at Broumana in the hills above Beirut in order to improve her Arabic. Although she appreciated her teacher, a Syrian who refused to let her pay for her books because he was so pleased she was learning his language, she found the atmosphere surrounding the mission stuffy and oppressive. "I've come to the conclusion I don't like missions," she wrote to her friend Venetia Buddicom in India. "I don't believe they are in any real touch with the people here, and feel they could have done so much better by just existing as a Christian school with no pretension to improve the heathen. It is extraordinary to see how little they manage to share the life of the place." With her usual

intrepidity, Freya soon began to undertake expeditions by herself, walking up and down the steep mule tracks to neighbouring villages. "These valleys", she wrote, "are so deep the sun never gets at them, I believe; you look up and see a rim of sunny villages about 2,000 feet over your head, and you walk in what looks like absolute solitude, until the voices of wood-cutters shouting out to each other the news of one solitary female wanderer make you

Freya Stark in Syria
aged 84

feel painfully conspicuous – the sort of feeling I remember in the war when being suddenly focused by a searchlight." Outside the mission she found the people charming and dignified, like the mountain people in Italy. "They are a fine-looking people too, magnificently built men, and women with eyes like stars." But they were also a "sad people. Neither Arab nor European. They could not stand independently of Europe against the Moslems of the interior. And if they hang on to Europe they are made the tool of every disgusting politician." Seeking a more authentic idea of the East, she moved to Damascus in March 1928 and lodged with a Syrian Christian family in the old city, having first unsuccessfully tried to find a Muslim family who would take her. In Damascus she found the lack of privacy discomforting. Her landlady, Sitt Rose, brought visitors into her room at all hours and made up her face in her mirror, using Freya's face powder. "I don't like my landlady here," she told Venetia. "She borrows my soap, and whenever we are out together, she gets into a carriage which I have to pay for . . . The trouble with travellers – and this includes missionaries – is that they come into contact with only the third or fourth rate people, and that gives no impression of *any* country." Freya was shocked by Rose's narrowness of mind – she had never visited the Great Mosque, one of the glories of the Syrian capital. She was much more impressed by the Muslims she met. A wealthy doctor who took her up into the hills surrounding Damascus and showed her his estates with a sweep of his arm, made her almost ecstatic. "It is a wonderful rich land," she wrote, "irrigated by the seven rivers which lose themselves in swamps full of duck and wild boars: all round are low volcanic hills. In spite of dust, noise, tawdriness, ugliness of detail, there is a magic: not to be understood in a day, or even two!"

In April Venetia Buddicom returned from India by way of Lebanon. The two women went by taxi to Damascus, stopping to view the magnificent Roman ruins at Baalbek, before setting out on what would prove to be Freya's first real adventure in the East: a trip to the Jebel Druze. This mountainous area south of Damascus was under martial law, following a two-year rebellion by the Druzes against the French mandatory government. The Druzes, a heterodox Shi'ite sect on the fringe of Islam, are a fiercely independent people. From the fifteenth to the eighteenth century they held sway over Mount Lebanon under a succession of dynasties within the wider frame of Ottoman rule, but throughout the 19th century they lost ground to the Maronite Christians who gained dominance with the help of their traditional allies, the French. In the competition between the Western powers that waxed with Ottoman decline, the British supported the Druzes; even today they tend to be a good deal more anglophile than other Middle Eastern communities. Once they reached the Syrian Druze heartland, two Inglizi ladies could be guaranteed a friendly reception. But to get there they had to evade the watchful eyes of the French.

Remains of Druze village destroyed by French forces 1925-6

This journey would set the pattern for the later travels in Persia and Southern Arabia on which Freya's reputation would be built. Although Venetia Buddicom came from a wealthy family, Freya herself was almost always short of funds. Unlike her famous predecessor, Gertrude Bell, who travelled with three baggage mules, two tents and three servants and ate alone in her tent, Freya made a virtue of necessity, preferring to enter into relations with the local people on a basis of social equality. She avoided officialdom, making her own arrangements through local contacts. In so doing she relied entirely on the goodwill and hospitality of the local people and on the protective attitude towards women prevailing at that time in Muslim lands. She repaid the hospitality she received with gifts – pen-knives or cigarette lighters bought in the city, or tourist souvenirs from Venice.

As an adventure, the expedition was a small triumph. On the third day Venetia and Freya were taken by local police to a French garrison, and were virtually placed under arrest. The French officers were astounded to find two young English women in their midst, and completely nonplussed. In evading the intelligence officer's questions Freya displayed all the charm and presence of mind that would characterize most of her subsequent dealings with authority. Claiming to be ordinary tourists, they blamed an out-of-date Thomas Cook guidebook

Venetia Buddicom with French officers Shahba 1928

for leading them astray. Freya hid the rifle belonging to Najm, their Druze guide, among the underclothes in her bag, relying on respect for female modesty to prevent its exposure. To his alarm and astonishment, she placed her diary, with its incriminating notes, in Najm's waistband. Soon the French soldiers were helping them on their way. Venetia's lovely blue eyes had been "almost too much" for the intelligence officer, and a Lieutenant – equally enslaved – volunteered to drive them to a local wedding. It was with a strong sense of satisfaction that they proceeded to Amman, capital of the Emirate of Transjordan, having outwitted the French. "It is so pleasant to feel that we have succeeded in doing what all the People who Know told us was impossible." They returned to Europe by way of Jerusalem and Cairo, following a more conventional tourist itinerary.

Freya returned to the Levant on many subsequent visits, usually travelling by boat and car. Lebanon was the gateway to Syria, as Syria was to Iraq; and she often began her expeditions to Southern Turkey from the comfort of one of Beirut's famous hotels. In 1933 she revisited Jordan, taking the old pilgrim

railway to Ma'an, in order to visit Petra, the ancient Nabatean city encased in pink sandstone hills above the Wadi 'Araba. She returned to Syria in 1939 to explore the castles of the legendary Assassins, and again in the mid-1950s. In later years she would prefer the city of Aleppo, with its labyrinthine covered *souk* and magificent citadel successively built by Hittites, Greeks and Muslims, to the more cosmopolitan and westernized

Euphrates raft with BBC film crew 1977

Damascus. Returning in 1954 after 15 years interrupted by war, she found it had lost none of its enchantment. "It is just the same as ever, and Aleppo the queen of cities this side of Isfahan."

Her last major expedition to the Levant was in May 1977 when she floated down the Euphrates on a raft made of reeds and inflated goatskins for the benefit of BBC television viewers. An unseasonal thunderstorm swamped the raft before it could be floated into the stream, and it was not until the goatskins had been replaced by oil drums that the craft became fully river-worthy. As they drifted with the current Freya conversed with her godson, Mark Lennox-Boyd, about the sweep of history and time, and the common impulses linking the conquests of Alexander the Great with the spread of the British Empire.

Freya writing on the raft 1977

In the shade of an umbrella, under a crimson hat, the bright intelligent eyes had lost none of their sparkle, the gently modulating voice, with its trace of a foreign accent, still conveyed a sense of wonder as she pointed to a passing mound or *tel* with "all the rubbish heaps of all the ages piling up!" Naive yet erudite, passionate yet cool, bohemian yet snobbish, Freya combined a romantic yearning for freedom with a classical impulse for order. Dwelling on her animated features the film caught some of those paradoxical qualities which, for all the books and letters that survive, have been lost with her passing.

For Freya Stark Lebanon was really the gateway to places further east or north, to Syria, Iraq and Turkey. Like Lady Hester Stanhope, the niece of William Pitt the Younger who abandoned London society to live and eventually to die in the East, she looked for the Other in that most exotic of regions which represented "space, distance, history and danger". She was most attracted to the 'pure' Arabs of the desert, or to mountain peoples uncontaminated by contact with European civilization. She admired the Druzes, with their secret religion and their wild, independent streak. The greatest of the Druze

Lady Diana Cooper at the grave of Lady Hester Stanhope, Djoun 1958

Emirs, Bashir II (1788-1840) built the beautiful Beit al-Din palace in the hills above Beirut. By the time Freya visited Lebanon, she decided it was "not the genuine Orient, only the semi-European fringe full of second-hand and second-rate, and European clothes and furniture peculiarly unadapted to the

Freya Stark with "B" Larsson, Beirut 1961

casual Eastern silhouette." She despised the cultural hybrids, whom she felt had abandoned their own way of life and values in order to espouse the dubious qualities of a modernity that inevitably came in European guise. The outlook represented by her Christian landlady in Brumana, Mlle Audi – "a gentle little thing with a sort of refined and faded youth still clinging to her" – seems to have annoyed her. "Here", she wrote, "it is too much, not too little civilization that is the trouble. That, and an incapacity for forgetting. Mlle Audi talks of iniquities of Druse governors two hundred years ago as if they had just happened." Similarly, she disliked Beirut, "a painfully Frankish town, (where) we go calling on each other in high heels and the Paris fashion last but one".

The great Roman Levantine city of Baalbek, where she stopped with Venetia Buddicom en route to Damascus in 1928, was a revelation. She could not fail to be impressed by the enormous blocks of stone supporting the massive columns of the Temple of Jupiter – the largest ever produced by classical antiquity. "One *feels* the size," she wrote, "acting harmoniously like strength"; so vast did it seem, that the tourists clambering over the ruins were reduced to the same scale as its normal residents – the swallows, hawks and lizards.

As she revisited Beirut in later years, Freya's attitude became more forgiving. Staying in luxury with her friend Moore Crosthwaite at the British Embassy in 1959, she reflected on the beauty of the coast "with its contrast of

H. St John Philby with Persian wife and sons, 1956

clustered houses and completely solitary gorges plunging down with tiers of rocks and pines". She even admired the city's rampant commercialism during what now seems a golden era before the civil war: "There is a gaiety and frankness about it which makes it rather pleasant!" The ultimate Temple of Mammon – the new Casino – was "going to be superb – a modern Baalbek with a terrace 380 meters long looking over the beautiful Bay of Juneh that rises like a wave in one long curving slope". Other friends she saw or stayed with in Lebanon included Barclay "B" Sanders, grand-daughter of her old friend Herbert Olivier, now married to Theo Larsson, a Swedish businessman; Diana Cooper, the famous 1920s beauty whose son John Julius Norwich was serving in the Embassy; and the Arabian explorer St John ("Jack") Philby, father of Kim Philby, the spy. When Freya met him in Beirut, Philby was living with his second wife Rozy (Firuza) and two sons in the village of Sannin above the Dog River (Nahr al-Kalb). During his sojourn in Arabia at the court of Ibn Saud, Philby had become a Muslim and married his second wife without divorcing his English wife, Dora. When Freya remarked that he seemed to be making the most of his new faith Philby explained that the King had presented Rozy to him, and he could hardly refuse a royal gift.

Above Beirut 1959

Djoun 1958

Sidon 1961

Near Broumana 1928

Sidon 1961

Beirut, St. George's Hotel 1957

Baalbek 1959

Beit el Din 1927

Mlle Audi at Broumana 1927

Orontes at Hermel 1958

Way to Djoun 1958

Tripoli Castle 1959

Pines near Broumana 1961

Tripoli 1959

Temple of Niha, Upper Beqa'a Valley 1954

Beirut 1957

When Freya first visited Damascus in 1928 she made friends with two young Muslim sisters Amat al-Latif and Ni'mat al 'Azm. She drove with them and their brother to the desert where she had her first encounter with real

bedouins living in goats-hair tents. "I never imagined that my first sight of the desert would come with such a shock of beauty and enslave me right away," she wrote. She despaired, however, of obtaining decent pictures: "All my photos of the day of the desert are bad," she complained to her mother, "there was no sun, and the terrific wind shook the camera." On her return to the city in 1929 the sisters drove her to Rihane in the Ghuta, the oasis of Damascus, where their uncle Najib al-Ghazi owned several villages and apricot plantations. Though she appreciated this experience of Muslim family life, Freya was struck by the social gulf between her hosts and the country people: "I believe the upper class people know as little of the bedouin and the peasants here as does the foreigner." She was equally dismissive

Ni'mat and Amat al-Latif al 'Azm

of the French administration: "It is ridiculous to call this a mandate, for I believe there is not a Frenchman in the country who intends these people ever to govern themselves."

In Syria the mainstream Sunni Muslims, whether rich or poor, lived mainly in the cities. The countryside, especially in the mountainous regions in the west and south, was mainly the province of Shi'a minorities – Druzes, Nusayris (also known as 'Alawis) and Ismailis. Freya's expedition to the Jebel Druze with Venetia Buddicom established two of the themes that would recur constantly in her writings: the natural dignity of country people for

whom life was harsh and precarious, and the endurance of antiquity. The Druzes had none of the comforts of modern civilization. There were no doctors and they harvested their meagre crops by the most primitive methods. Yet they were handsome, tough and dignified, holding firmly to the canons of a faith which they very sensibly kept to themselves. At Shahba

Druze Sheikh al 'Aql (senior cleric) Ahmad Al Hajari, Qanawat 1928

and Resas, 'Atyl and Qanawat, and in the villages east of Aleppo, the peasants inhabited ancient sites that had once been small jewels in the crown of the Hellenistic, Roman and Byzantine empires. The contrast between past glories and present poverty can be seen in many of the photographs where beautifully carved masonry is juxtaposed with baked mud and thatch, and columns that once graced the courtyards of temples and cloisters are now used to prop up rustic walls and roofs.

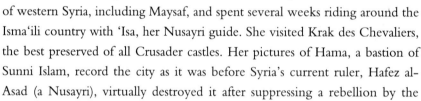

Freya returned to Syria in summer 1939 just before the outbreak of war. In Aleppo she stayed with the Altounians, an Irish-Armenian family who had known T. E. Lawrence. After her now famous expedition to the stronghold of Alamut in Persia, described in *The Valleys of the Assassins*, she wanted to explore the Isma'ili castles of western Syria, including Maysaf, and spent several weeks riding around the Isma'ili country with 'Isa, her Nusayri guide. She visited Krak des Chevaliers, the best preserved of all Crusader castles. Her pictures of Hama, a bastion of Sunni Islam, record the city as it was before Syria's current ruler, Hafez al-Asad (a Nusayri), virtually destroyed it after suppressing a rebellion by the Muslim Brotherhood in 1981. However, the giant *naouras* or water-wheels which have fed the irrigation canals since medieval times survive.

Freya (in hat) and her Druze guide Najm (with umbrella), Jebel Druze 1928

After the Second World War Freya made several more journeys in Syria. In May 1956 she explored the deserted Byzantine cities of the Orontes Valley, east of Antioch (Antakya, now in Turkey). She visited about twenty separate sites of what were once the summer resorts of Antioch merchants, looking back to the time when the hills were still covered with vines and olives. "All the comfort and luxury and civilisation seem to hover there, though lost in Antioch itself. But it has grown so faint that it only comes back to those who give it time, and do not hurry on the road in cars, but ride slowly from ruin to ruin, letting the country and all the meaning sink in slowly."

The Altounian family, Aleppo 1956

Palmyra 1937

Near Hama 1937

Damascus, Ghuta Oasis 1929

Euphrates Ferry at Sirrin 1937

Aleppo 1956

Deir Sim'an 1936

Najib al Ghazi, Rihane, Damascus 1929

Watchman, Aleppo 1939

Frontier guard 1930

Orontes east of Aleppo 1939

'Alleiqa 1939

Water-filled goatskins 1933

Collecting raisins, Rihane, Damascus 1929

Redeme 1928

Druze Sheikh 1928

'Alleiqa 1939

Ibrahim bin Ahmed al Hajari with his son
Hussein, Qanawat 1928

Jebel Druze 1928

'Isa, Nusayri guide, 1939

Above Safita 1939

Ismailis from Al Qaf 1939

Young Ismaili 1939

Aleppo to Euphrates 1939

Garden of Saladin's tomb Damascus 1928

Near Sirrin 1939

Women's howdah near Damascus 1928

Making butter, Alleiqa 1939

Near Sirrin 1939

Apamea (Qal'at al Mudīq) 1939

Krak des Chevaliers (Qal'at al Husn) 1939

Safita 1939

Ismaili girl 1939

Acolyte, Hama 1939

"Lear's Fool" 'Alleiqa 1939. The man followed Freya and her party, laughing at everything.

Euphrates ferryman 1939

Harvest, Euphrates bank 1939

Latakia 1939

Tartous 1939

Sheizar 1939

Aleppo Castle 1954

'Atyl 1928

Serjibleh 1956

Deir Sim'an 1956

Deir Simʻan 1956

Refadeh 1956

Deir Sim'an 1956

Baqirha 1956

Jebel Barisha 1956

Baqirha 1956

Krak des Chevaliers 1939

Refadeh 1956

Damascus 1928

Hama 1939

Hama 1939

Village near Aleppo 1956

Euphrates 1939

Maysaf 1939

Bridge over the Orontes at Sheizar 1939

Hama 1939

Hama 1939

Dar Quita to Babiska 1956

Deir Sim'an 1956

Refadeh 1956

Villes Mortes 1956

Krak des Chevaliers 1939

Maysaf 1939

Sahiun 1939

Ismaili country near Al Qaf 1939

Way to Al Qaf 1939

Outside Damascus 1928

Near Hama 1928

After the expedition to the Jebel Druze in 1928 Freya drove briefly through what was then Transjordan on her way to Jerusalem. The gentle wooded valleys around the Saracen castle of Ajlun came as a relief after the black basalt desert south of Damascus. "We went through very lovely rich country, deep valley cuts and up again among hills; gradually to trees and real woods, through corn waving in loneliness, so that one wonders who comes to reap

Stewart Perowne and Sir Alec Kirkbride, Amman 1943

here." She made her first proper visit to the Emirate in March 1933, driving for two days and nights across the desert from Baghdad in a lorry carrying a load of fish, accompanied by a Russian driver, his Arab assistant and a Swiss professor of philology. The latter appeared to be something of a caricature, "with black beard, glasses, soft hat and peculiar buccaneering clothes finished off with a white shirt and what looked like an evening collar – and a note-book always ready". When they reached the frontier at Azraq, Freya determined to visit Old Azraq, a small oasis nearby. The driver was cajoled into taking the truck with all its contents and passengers on a sightseeing tour. No sooner had they reached the hollow with its black basalt fort than the truck became stuck. While the villagers – mostly Druze refugees from the rebellion in Syria – pulled it out, Freya went to work with her camera.

On her first visit to Amman in 1933 the Emir Abdullah's capital was little more than a village. Freya took pride in the part played by Britain in setting up the Emirate after the First World War: "One can't help feeling pleased at being English when seeing this peaceful holding of the land, the police and roads, and air routes, where before there were only desert raiders." On passing through the city in 1943 she visited two of the architects of this Pax Britannica, Sir John Bagot Glubb (Glubb Pasha) and the High Commissioner, Sir Alec Kirkbride. As founder of the bedouin police and the Arab Legion, Glubb had welded the country's warring tribes into a force that would support the

Glubb Pasha and family, Amman 1943

91

Hashemite Emir – and Britain's interests. Kirkbride exercised his diplomatic sway from the British Residency next to the Emir Abdullah's palace.

On her 1933 trip Freya and the Swiss professor took the train to the southern town of Ma'an – a leisurely eight hours along the famous Hejaz railway built by the Germans before the First World War and regularly sabotaged by T. E. Lawrence and his Arab raiders. Here they hired a car and driver, and drove some 20 miles to Ras al-Naqb where the 4,000-foot Arabian plateau falls away suddenly, leaving a fantastic archipelago of rocks in a sea of sand and hard-baked mud. From here they could see the massive walls of Wadi Rum, where Lawrence camped among the Huweitat bedouin – and where David Lean would shoot some of the battle scenes for "Lawrence of Arabia". It was not until 1961, however, that Freya found a jeep to drive her into Wadi Rum, courtesy of the Save the Children Fund, which held a regular clinic there.

Transjordan police truck 1933

Freya and her professor returned by way of Abu Lisan, scene of one of Lawrence's most famous battles, and then drove west to Wadi Musa, where, perforce, they had to act like other tourists, paying for the services of a policeman, bedouin porters and a tired old horse for the walk into Petra. When Johan Burckhardt, the Swiss explorer, became the first modern European to visit Petra in 1812 he dressed as an Arab and had to sacrifice a goat. By 1933 the ancient city, created by the Nabatean Arabs who controlled the spice routes during the early centuries of the Christian era, was firmly on the tourist map. Thomas Cook made a camp at the head of the canyon where visitors could choose to sleep in a tent or a cave. Freya found the façades to be in "rather bad taste". The Nabateans, she wrote, "must have been a horrid rich commercial people, all out for display, and with a very coarse taste in their sculpture".

Wadi Rum Police Post 1961

Azraq 1933

Druze women, Azraq 1933

Ajlun Castle 1943

Wadi Musa 1933

Desert Police Wadi Rum 1961

Thomas Cook Camp, Petra 1933

Bedouin boy in Save the Children Fund clothes, by Nabatean temple, Wadi Rum, 1961

Overlooking Wadi Rum 1933

Amman 1933

Amman 1961

Petra 1933 – "The Treasury"

Petra 1933 – Entrance to the gorge

Petra 1933 – Older Nabatean Tombs

Wellesley Bombers over Jordan 1943 [photo Charles E. Brown]

Freya's first visit to Jerusalem in 1928 left her unimpressed. Having stayed in Damascus and visited the Jebel Druze, she found it rather suburban. Determined to build a reputation as a traveller she was less than enthusiastic about a place which drew western visitors in their hundreds, if not thousands. "We shall be rather glad to leave," she informed her mother after only three days in the Holy City. "What with packing, mending, finding our luggage, getting money &c, we are being reduced to the harassed state of mind of the ordinary tourist." She and Venetia had crossed into Palestine by the Allenby Bridge near Jericho in the heat of May. Climbing through the hot baked rock to the western side of the Jordan Valley, they came across the city suddenly, with "all its varieties of architecture and beliefs gathered in the squareness of the medieval walls". "It was impressive in an unexpected way and in spite of all the ugly detail," she added grudgingly. On returning to Jerusalem from Baghdad in April 1933, however, she was in a rather more benign mood. She stayed at the American School of Archaeology, where she found a "sort of ascetic comradely feeling about the place". Nothing could take away from Jerusalem "her magnificent position and clear beautiful atmosphere".

Bridge of the Daughters of Jacob on the Syria-Palestine frontier 1928

Freya's pictures of Acre were taken in June 1931. She had sailed to Haifa from Venice on her way to Baghdad and spent a morning looking round the old Arab town with its famous Crusader castle. She liked the way the mosques and houses revealed themselves above the walls; but the walls themselves were a disappointment, having been regularly rebuilt – enough to withstand the famous siege by Napoleon Bonaparte in 1799.

Freya revisited Palestine on many occasions during the Second World War, stopping in Jerusalem on her journeys between Cairo and Baghdad. She usually visited Government House, a fine modern building set apart from the city, designed by the architect Austen Harrison. Here the British High Commissioner, Sir Harold MacMichael, and his wife had created an oasis of calm amidst the turmoil of war. "It was (or seemed to the visitor) a haven at that time, between eastern and western anxieties of Hitler's pincer movement; and a refreshment to see terraces of lavender and rosemary with Nesta MacMichael planning herbaceous borders, in a deceptive landscape of stability that sloped between the stones."

Sir Harold MacMichael on the terrace of Government House, Jerusalem, 1943

A firm believer in the virtues of the British Empire (as distinct from the French and Italian varieties), Freya Stark was a keen defender of the system of mandates established after the First World War to prepare Palestine, Transjordan and Iraq for independence. Like most of her fellow-Arabists, she was strongly opposed to Zionist settlement in Palestine which accelerated during the 1930s as the persecution of Jews in Europe gathered pace. She admired the Jews for their enterprise, however, and defended herself against accusations of anti-semitism. The inter-war period saw the Jewish population of Palestine increase tenfold, from around 50,000 to close on half a million. This dramatic shift in the demography provoked the full-scale Arab revolt in 1936 which the British put down with considerable severity. A Royal Commission recommended partition of Palestine into Arab and Jewish states. The proposal met with such opposition from the Arabs, at a time when their support was deemed to be crucial, that it was overruled. Instead, the Colonial Secretary, Malcolm MacDonald, produced a White Paper limiting Jewish immigration according to the "economic absorptive capacity" of the country – which at the outbreak of war was fixed at 29,000. In the autumn of 1943 Freya was sent to the United States by the Ministry of Information to defend the White Paper against the Zionists, who demanded unrestricted immigration to Palestine. In the light of the revelations emerging from Eastern Europe her task was a hopeless one, but she performed it with characteristic humour and panache.

Jerusalem, Nebi Musa Pilgrimage 1933

Jerusalem, Haram Al Sharif 1933

Jerusalem, Dome of the Rock 1933

Near Nazareth 1930

Acre 1931

Acre 1931

Acre Mosque 1931

Jerusalem 1933

Jerusalem 1961

Palestine Mounted Policeman 1933

CHRONOLOGY

1893 Born January 31st in Paris to Robert and Flora Stark.

1894 Sister Vera born.

1906 Loses part of her scalp in accident in Italian carpet factory.

1911 Enters Bedford College, London, boarding with Viva Jeyes. Meets Professor W. P. Ker who becomes her mentor. Robert Stark leaves his family and emigrates to Canada. Flora Stark remains in Italy.

1914 On the outbreak of war works briefly in the censorship department before volunteering as a nurse in G. M. Trevelyan's Italian ambulance unit.

1915 Serves in hospitals near Italian-Austrian front. Witnesses famous Italian retreat from Caporetto.

1921 Begins learning Arabic from her home at La Mortela near Genoa.

1923 Death of W. P. Ker while climbing with F.S. on Monte Rosa.

1926 Herbert Young, a friend of her father's, makes her his heir to the Casa Freia at Asolo, the Venetian hill town which becomes her home. Vera dies of septicaemia, following a miscarriage, leaving four young children.

1927 Enrols at the School of Oriental and African Studies in London to continue Arabic classes.

1927 December-March 1928. Spends winter in Broumana, near Beirut, improving Arabic.

1928 Visits Damascus. Expedition to Jebel Druze with Venetia Buddicom. Returns to Italy via Transjordan, Palestine and Egypt.

1929 Arrives in Baghdad.

1930-1 Visits Castles of the Assassins, and travels through Western Persia.

1932 *Baghdad Sketches* published by *Baghdad Times*.

1933 Travels in Persia earn the Royal Geographical Society's Back Memorial Grant.

1934 *Valleys of the Assassins* published to critical acclaim.

1935 First journey to the Hadhramaut in South Arabia (now Yemen).

1936 *The Southern Gates of Arabia* published.

1938 Wakefield Expedition to Hadhramaut with archaeologist Gertrude Caton Thompson.

1939 April-May: visits Crusader Castles in Syria. September: sent to Aden as assistant to Stewart Perowne in Government Information Department.

1940 February: travels to Sana'a, the Yemeni capital, to counter pro-Axis influence. June: Italy enters war - Sana'a remains neutral. September: transferred to Cairo. October: *Winter in Arabia* published. December: begins work recruiting Egyptians for anti-Axis "Brotherhood of Freedom".

1941 Divides time between Cairo and Baghdad, where she establishes Iraqi branch of the Brotherhood. May: endures siege of British Embassy by nationalist government of Rashid Ali al Gailani. Remains mostly in Baghdad till July 1942.

1942 April: visits Northern Iraq and Iraqi Kurdistan. July-October: on leave in Cyprus. Encouraged by Sir Sidney Cockerell begins work on first volume of autobiography *Traveller's Prelude*. November: Flora Stark dies in the USA. *Letter from Syria*, based on 1927-8 travels in Levant, published. Receives Founder's Gold Medal from Royal Geographic Society for travels in South Arabia.

1943 February-March: Visits Wavells in India. Drives back through Persia, selling government car at considerable profit in Tehran. October-June 1944: tours USA to defend British policy of restricting Jewish immigration into Palestine.

1944 August-January 1945: stays in England, writing *East is West*.

1945	February: flies to India to work with Lady Wavell in mustering support for Empire among Indian women. May 3rd VE Day. July: returns to Casa Freia in Asolo. Works for Ministry of Information setting up reading centres in Italy under auspices of Allied Military Government.
1947	October: marries Stewart Perowne.
1948	February: joins Perowne in Barbados, where he was Deputy Governor. July: returns to Italy and remains in Europe apart from visit to West Indies in December-March 1949. *Perseus in the Wind*, essays, published.
1950	March: joins Perowne in Libya where he has been appointed Adviser to new government of King Idris. *Traveller's Prelude* published. Visits Greece.
1951	March: returns to Asolo, deciding marriage is over. Honorary Degree from Glasgow University. *Beyond Euphrates* (autobiography vol. II), published.
1952	Marriage dissolved. Autumn: travels in Greece and Turkey.
1953	June: awarded CBE in Coronation Honours. *Coast of Incense* (autobiography vol. III) published.
1954	March-August: travels in Syria, Turkey and Greece. *Ionia: A Quest* published.
1956	May-July: visits "lost" Byzantine cities in Northern Syria and Southern Turkey. *The Lycian Shore* published.
1957	Autumn: visits Turkey, Mosul and Baghdad.
1958	July-August: visits Northern and Central Turkey. *Alexander's Path* published.
1959	Visits Iran, Greece, Lebanon and Kenya. *Riding to the Tigris* published.
1960	Visits Tunisia, Greece and Turkey
1961	Visits Cambodia, China, India, Turkey, Lebanon and Egypt. *Dust in the Lion's Paw* (autobiography vol. IV) published.
1962	Visits central Turkey.
1963	Visits Istanbul. *The Journey's Echo* - an anthology, published.
1964	Begins building Montoria, new house outside Asolo.
1966	Sells Casa Freia to Asolo municipality. Visits Greece and Turkey. *Rome on the Euphrates* published.
1967	September: visits Afghanistan, Samarkand, Bukhara and Tashkent.
1968	Visits Afghanistan and Greece. *The Zodiac Arch*, anthology, published.
1970	November: visits Nepal. *The Minaret of Djam* published.
1972	Becomes Dame of the British Empire in New Year's Honours.
1973	Sells Montoria, moves to flat in Asolo. Visits Kashmir.
1975	Visits Bodrum and Istanbul in Turkey.
1976	March: visits Sana'a, North Yemen and Southern Turkey. Stays with Queen Mother in Castle of Mey. *A Peak in Darien*, essays, published.
1977	To Syria with BBC television crew for journey down the Euphrates on specially constructed raft.
1984	Revisits Nepal with BBC television crew.
1985	Receives Freedom of the City of Asolo.
1993	31 January: celebrates 100th birthday.
1993	9 May: dies at her home in Asolo.

All of Freya Stark's books are published by John Murray with the exception of eight volumes of letters edited by Lucy and Caroline Moorehead, published by Michael Russell between 1974 and 1982. A book of photographs of South Arabia, *Seen in the Hadhramaut*, appeared in 1938. *Over the Rim of the World*, a selection of letters edited by Caroline Moorehead, published by Murrays in association with Michael Russell, appeared in 1988. Books about Freya Stark include *A Tower in the Wall* by Alexander Maitland (Blackwood 1982), *Traveller Through Time* by Malise Ruthven (Viking 1986), *Freya Stark* by Caroline Moorehead (Penguin 1986) and *Freya Stark – a biography* by Molly Izzard (Hodder & Stoughton 1993).